Your Personal
DREAM JOURNAL

OPENING DOORS TO YOUR FUTURE,
FREEDOM & LIFE OF VICTORY

Melbourne, Florida USA

Your Personal Dream Journal
Perfect Bound Edition

© 2018 by Sandie Freed.

Published by Parsons Publishing House
P. O. Box 410063
Melbourne, Florida 32941 USA
www.ParsonsPublishingHouse.com
Info@ParsonsPublishingHouse.com

All rights reserved. This book or parts thereof may not be reproduced in any form, stored in a retrieval system, or transmitted in any form by any means—electronic, mechanical, photocopy, recording or otherwise—without prior written permission of the publisher, except as provided by the United States copyright law.

ISBN-13: 978-160273-103-5
ISBN-10: 1-60273-103-9
Printed in the United States of America.
For World-Wide Distribution.

INTRODUCTION

What convinced you to start using a dream journal? There are many reasons you might opt to keep a dream journal: peculiar dreams that beckon you, haunting dreams that menace you, and possibly fantastical dreams that mesmerize you. Dreams, by their very nature, are curious and mysterious. Excluding the Gospel message, only in your dreams can someone who was dead live again; someone you recognize suddenly becomes someone else, animals become people, or people become animals. It's only in dreams where all the physical laws on this earth can be broken.

I believe you were drawn to this journal to record God's messages to you, His beloved child. To be sure, God, our Heavenly Father, is a great and caring father. In His magnificence and holiness, He reaches out to draw us closer to Him. From the Garden of Eden, God has sought after and longed for intimacy with man. Even with regard to the sin wall that Adam erected when he sinned, God reached through the blood of Jesus to bring forgiveness and closeness once again. Join me now on this adventure in journaling and interpreting your dreams; you don't want to miss your next appointment with destiny.

God Still Speaks Today

Even this day, the Lord continues to speak through dreams and visions. It's important to remember that when God speaks, He will never contradict or violate His Word. The Bible is inerrant and unchanging and should serve as our north star to guide us as we are being molded into God's image. If you dream about being married to your neighbor's spouse, be assured that the dream is not from God; it violates God's laws and nature.

Over and over in the Bible, there are stories that emphasize this communication as being every bit real as it is supernatural. Though the record of occurrences goes back millennia, science remains mystified as to the purpose of dreams and visions. Today's church lends no claim as to all dreams being from God; however, it is a surety that this means is utilized by the Almighty to edify, exhort, and comfort His people. God wants to bring you close and communicate with you, and He wants to do that through dreams and visions.

Why Keep a Dream Journal?

As I referenced earlier, there are many different reasons why one chooses to keep a dream journal. With all kinds of electrodes and studies, science proves that low levels of neurotransmitters and electrical activity in the brain, which are responsible for long-term memory, are found to be in low levels upon awakening. With that knowledge, a bedside dream journal has proven to be a great aid in remembering dreams.

Also, keeping a journal will allow you to categorize your dreams and discern patterns that might exist. Patterns can lead to the unfolding of an intricate truth that God is wanting to reveal. As I shared in chapter 12 of Understanding Your Dreams (Chosen, 2017), God unfolded a life-changing series of dreams that exposed a generational curse which brought me complete freedom. My dream journal helped me understand the full scope of what God was revealing.
We see in Daniel 7:1 that Daniel wrote the dream. Keeping an active dream journal will help keep you accountable to God. It will also help you build your faith. As you see how God has faithfully spoken to you over the years, you will trust Him once again in the midst of a battle.

The main reason I use a journal is to document my dreams so that I can pray over them. Journaling your dreams is priceless.

Wake Up

As humans, we each spend at least one third of our lives sleeping – totaling eight years or more. In those sleeping hours, we may have three to five dreams per night. For a child of God, this gives great opportunity for God to speak secrets to you that only you will understand. You will find that it's possible to train yourself to remember your dreams once you awaken. Experiment with different methods and continue to use the ones that work. It's best to teach yourself to wake up after dreaming; however, if you don't awaken, spend some quiet reflective time to examine any dreams you may recall the following morning. Once you wake up, don't move and make an opportunity to remember the dream details. Then, write them in your journal.

How to Use a Journal

We have designed this special ministry dream journal to prompt you to remember certain important things about your dream. The labels guide you to observe certain colors, key symbols, the people, the time, etc. All of these things will help you as you begin to interpret your dream. One thing is sure, if you cannot remember your dream, you will not have to worry about interpreting it. It's important to remember that all dreams are not from God and writing them down will help you make that determination. Pray and God will lead you by your inner man to determine the origin of any of your dreams.

When you awake from a dream, immediately document symbols, scenes, people, etc. Take notice of the sequence of events as you record your emotions during and after the dream. In the middle of the night, you may only write down the symbols that will trigger your full recollection in the morning.

Interpreting Dreams

Become extremely familiar with biblical accounts of dreams and visions in addition to the principles upon which God Himself operates; He will always stay true to them.

There are two important things to remember when interpreting dreams:

1) Nothing is always – A symbol will never mean the same thing every time.
2) Remember who the Holy Spirit is – The Spirit will lead and guide you according to the Bible.

You can consult my book entitled ***Understanding Your Dreams*** (Chosen, 2017) and the ***Dreams Companion Study Guide*** (Parsons Publishing House, 2018) to gain more insight on dream interpretation. In my book on dreams, I include my 40-page dictionary on symbolism that can show you what some widely used symbols represent. This dictionary is just a guide and should never be used exclusively.

As you become more experienced with dream interpretation, you will see a pattern emerge of how God speaks to you. This will help you build your own personal dream language. The symbols in your dreams are meant for you, and God will use this personal vocabulary to speak mysteries to you in the night seasons. As I said earlier, your Bible and the Holy Spirit will lead you to the true interpretation of your dream; the next most important thing is your personal dream language.

	DREAM INTERPRETATION HELPS
1	Not all dreams are from God.
2	Most dreams are not to be taken literally and need interpretation.
3	The Holy Spirit is the ultimate guide and teacher of proper interpretation.
4	Dreams are always to be considered on a personal basis first, rather than assuming the dream is about someone else.
5	God will often speak in familiar terms. He will even use your own phrases and jokes.
6	Always write down your dream upon awakening. A dream journal gives a central place for recording. Give the dream a title and a date.
7	Take time to ponder your dream and allow the Holy Spirit to lead you. Do not rush the interpretation.
8	Reduce your dream to the simplest form—keep the main thing the main thing! Ask yourself if there is a central theme. Is a main thought, issue or particular word mentioned several times?
9	Take note of how you felt when you awoke—angry, fearful, excited?
10	Note if you had a nightmare or awoke to an evil presence in the room. This could have been a demonic dream.
11	Awakening from a dream to a heavenly atmosphere often indicates that an angel brought a dream to you and the angelic presence is still abiding.
12	Consecutive dreams often connect similar meanings. God frequently speaks the same message in different ways and with different symbolism.
13	Note the colors in the dream. Is the dream completely in black and white or in vivid colors, such as green and red? Note the main color throughout the dream.
14	Is there more than one theme in the dream? Quite often God will give several themes in one dream.
15	Many dreams are for the future and can only be understood as they unfold over a period of time. Again, do not rush the interpretation. Patience is a virtue in dream interpretation.
16	Dreams may be for you personally or to guide you in prayer and intercession for church, city, national and international issues.
17	Ask! Ask! And ask again! Dream interpretation comes from asking God for answers.

Your Personal Dream Journal

Sandie Freed

My Dream

Date: ⬤ Time: ⬤ Recurring? ⬤ When? ⬤
Dream Title:
⬤

Main Character: ⬤ Self   ⬤ Other: _____
Your Role: ⬤ Participant ⬤ Observer
Colors: ⬤ B&W   ⬤ Vivid   ⬤ Muted   Color/s: _____

Location: _____

What's in the Background? _____

Emotions During the Dream: | Emotions Upon Awakening:
  ⬤ Fear   ⬤ Dread | ⬤ Fear   ⬤ Dread
  ⬤ Joy   ⬤ Excitement | ⬤ Joy   ⬤ Excitement
  ⬤ Other_____ | ⬤ Other_____

What's the Dream About?

List or Sketch Important Symbols

Pray for the Interpretation

Your Personal Dream Journal

My Reflections

Continued

Notable Events Going on at this Time

Sandie Freed

My Dream

Date: _____ Time: _____ Recurring? _____ When? _____
Dream Title: _____

Main Character: ● Self   ● Other: _____
Your Role: ● Participant ● Observer
Colors: ● B&W   ● Vivid   ● Muted   Color/s: _____

Location: _____

What's in the Background? _____

Emotions During the Dream: Emotions Upon Awakening:
  ● Fear   ● Dread   ● Fear   ● Dread
  ● Joy   ● Excitement   ● Joy   ● Excitement
  ● Other_____   ● Other_____

What's the Dream About?

List or Sketch Important Symbols

Pray for the Interpretation

11

Your Personal Dream Journal

My Reflections

Continued

Notable Events Going on at this Time

Sandie Freed

My Dream

Date: _____ Time: _____ Recurring? _____ When? _____
Dream Title:
_____

Main Character: ● Self   ● Other: _____
Your Role: ● Participant   ● Observer
Colors: ● B&W   ● Vivid   ● Muted   Color/s: _____

Location: _____

What's in the Background? _____

Emotions During the Dream:	Emotions Upon Awakening:
● Fear ● Dread	● Fear ● Dread
● Joy ● Excitement	● Joy ● Excitement
● Other_____	● Other_____

What's the Dream About?

List or Sketch Important Symbols

Pray for the Interpretation

Your Personal Dream Journal

My Reflections

Continued

Notable Events Going on at this Time

Sandie Freed

My Dream

Date: _____ Time: _____ Recurring? _____ When? _____
Dream Title:
_____

Main Character: ● Self   ● Other: _____
Your Role: ● Participant ● Observer
Colors: ● B&W   ● Vivid   ● Muted   Color/s: _____

Location: _____

What's in the Background? _____

Emotions During the Dream:	Emotions Upon Awakening:
● Fear ● Dread	● Fear ● Dread
● Joy ● Excitement	● Joy ● Excitement
● Other_____	● Other_____

What's the Dream About?

List or Sketch Important Symbols

Pray for the Interpretation

Your Personal Dream Journal

My Reflections

Continued

Notable Events Going on at this Time

Sandie Freed

My Dream

Date: ▓▓▓   Time: ▓▓▓   Recurring? ▓▓▓   When? ▓▓▓

Dream Title: ▓▓▓▓▓▓▓▓▓▓▓▓▓▓▓▓▓▓▓▓▓▓▓▓▓▓

Main Character: ● Self   ● Other: _____
Your Role: ● Participant ● Observer
Colors: ● B&W   ● Vivid   ● Muted   Color/s: _____

Location: _____

What's in the Background? _____

Emotions During the Dream:	Emotions Upon Awakening:
● Fear ● Dread	● Fear ● Dread
● Joy ● Excitement	● Joy ● Excitement
● Other_____	● Other_____

What's the Dream About?

List or Sketch Important Symbols

Pray for the Interpretation

Your Personal Dream Journal

My Reflections

Continued

Notable Events Going on at this Time

Sandie Freed

My Dream

Date: ▬▬▬ Time: ▬▬▬ Recurring? ▬▬▬ When? ▬▬▬
Dream Title:
▬▬▬▬▬▬▬▬▬▬▬▬▬▬▬▬▬▬▬▬▬▬

Main Character: ● Self   ● Other: _____
Your Role: ● Participant ● Observer
Colors: ● B&W   ● Vivid   ● Muted   Color/s: _____

Location: _____

What's in the Background? _____

Emotions During the Dream: | Emotions Upon Awakening:
  ● Fear   ● Dread | ● Fear   ● Dread
  ● Joy   ● Excitement | ● Joy   ● Excitement
  ● Other_____ | ● Other_____

What's the Dream About?

List or Sketch Important Symbols

Pray for the Interpretation

Your Personal Dream Journal

My Reflections

Continued

Notable Events Going on at this Time

Sandie Freed

My Dream

Date: ⬤   Time: ⬤   Recurring? ⬤   When? ⬤
Dream Title:

Main Character: ⬤ Self   ⬤ Other: _____
Your Role: ⬤ Participant   ⬤ Observer
Colors: ⬤ B&W   ⬤ Vivid   ⬤ Muted   Color/s: _____

Location: _____

What's in the Background? _____

Emotions During the Dream: Emotions Upon Awakening:
  ⬤ Fear   ⬤ Dread   ⬤ Fear   ⬤ Dread
  ⬤ Joy   ⬤ Excitement   ⬤ Joy   ⬤ Excitement
  ⬤ Other_____   ⬤ Other_____

What's the Dream About?

List or Sketch Important Symbols

Pray for the Interpretation

Your Personal Dream Journal

My Reflections

Continued

Notable Events Going on at this Time

Sandie Freed

My Dream

Date: ▔▔▔▔▔ Time: ▔▔▔▔ Recurring? ▔▔▔▔ When? ▔▔▔▔
Dream Title:
▔▔▔▔▔▔▔▔▔▔▔▔▔▔▔▔▔▔▔▔▔▔▔▔▔▔▔▔▔▔▔▔▔▔▔▔

Main Character: ● Self   ● Other: _____
Your Role: ● Participant   ● Observer
Colors: ● B&W   ● Vivid   ● Muted   Color/s: _____

Location: _____

What's in the Background? _____

Emotions During the Dream:	Emotions Upon Awakening:
● Fear ● Dread	● Fear ● Dread
● Joy ● Excitement	● Joy ● Excitement
● Other_____	● Other_____

What's the Dream About?

List or Sketch Important Symbols

Pray for the Interpretation

Your Personal Dream Journal

My Reflections

Continued

Notable Events Going on at this Time

Sandie Freed

My Dream

Date: _____ Time: _____ Recurring? _____ When? _____
Dream Title:
_____

Main Character: ● Self   ● Other: _____
Your Role: ● Participant ● Observer
Colors: ● B&W   ● Vivid   ● Muted   Color/s: _____

Location: _____

What's in the Background? _____

Emotions During the Dream: Emotions Upon Awakening:
  ● Fear   ● Dread   ● Fear   ● Dread
  ● Joy   ● Excitement   ● Joy   ● Excitement
  ● Other_____   ● Other_____

What's the Dream About?

List or Sketch Important Symbols

Pray for the Interpretation

Your Personal Dream Journal

My Reflections

Continued

Notable Events Going on at this Time

Sandie Freed

My Dream

Date: _____ Time: _____ Recurring? _____ When? _____
Dream Title:
_____

Main Character: ● Self   ● Other: _____
Your Role: ● Participant ● Observer
Colors: ● B&W   ● Vivid   ● Muted   Color/s: _____

Location: _____

What's in the Background? _____

Emotions During the Dream:	Emotions Upon Awakening:
● Fear ● Dread	● Fear ● Dread
● Joy ● Excitement	● Joy ● Excitement
● Other_____	● Other_____

What's the Dream About?

List or Sketch Important Symbols

Pray for the Interpretation

Your Personal Dream Journal

My Reflections

Continued

Notable Events Going on at this Time

Sandie Freed

My Dream

Date: _____ Time: _____ Recurring? _____ When? _____
Dream Title:
_____

Main Character: ● Self   ● Other: _____
Your Role: ● Participant ● Observer
Colors: ● B&W   ● Vivid   ● Muted   Color/s: _____

Location: _____

What's in the Background? _____

Emotions During the Dream: | Emotions Upon Awakening:
● Fear   ● Dread | ● Fear   ● Dread
● Joy   ● Excitement | ● Joy   ● Excitement
● Other_____ | ● Other_____

What's the Dream About?

List or Sketch Important Symbols

Pray for the Interpretation

Your Personal Dream Journal

My Reflections

Continued

Notable Events Going on at this Time

Sandie Freed

My Dream

Date: ▢　　　Time: ▢　　　Recurring? ▢　　　When? ▢
Dream Title:
▢

Main Character:　● Self　　　● Other: _____
Your Role:　　　● Participant　● Observer
Colors: ● B&W　● Vivid　　　● Muted　Color/s: _____

Location: _____

What's in the Background? _____

Emotions During the Dream:	Emotions Upon Awakening:
● Fear　● Dread	● Fear　● Dread
● Joy　● Excitement	● Joy　● Excitement
● Other_____	● Other_____

What's the Dream About?

List or Sketch Important Symbols

Pray for the Interpretation

Your Personal Dream Journal

My Reflections

Continued

Notable Events Going on at this Time

Sandie Freed

My Dream

Date: _____ Time: _____ Recurring? _____ When? _____
Dream Title:
_____

Main Character: ● Self   ● Other: _____
Your Role: ● Participant ● Observer
Colors: ● B&W   ● Vivid   ● Muted   Color/s: _____

Location: _____

What's in the Background? _____

Emotions During the Dream:	Emotions Upon Awakening:
● Fear ● Dread	● Fear ● Dread
● Joy ● Excitement	● Joy ● Excitement
● Other_____	● Other_____

What's the Dream About?

List or Sketch Important Symbols

Pray for the Interpretation

Your Personal Dream Journal

My Reflections

Continued

Notable Events Going on at this Time

Sandie Freed

My Dream

Date: _____ Time: _____ Recurring? _____ When? _____
Dream Title:
_____

Main Character: ● Self   ● Other: _____
Your Role: ● Participant   ● Observer
Colors: ● B&W   ● Vivid   ● Muted   Color/s: _____

Location: _____

What's in the Background? _____

Emotions During the Dream:	Emotions Upon Awakening:
● Fear ● Dread	● Fear ● Dread
● Joy ● Excitement	● Joy ● Excitement
● Other_____	● Other_____

What's the Dream About?

List or Sketch Important Symbols

Pray for the Interpretation

Your Personal Dream Journal

My Reflections

Continued

Notable Events Going on at this Time

Sandie Freed

My Dream

Date: ▇▇▇ Time: ▇▇▇ Recurring? ▇▇▇ When? ▇▇▇
Dream Title:
▇▇▇▇▇▇▇▇▇▇▇▇▇▇▇▇▇▇▇▇▇▇▇▇▇▇▇▇▇▇▇▇

Main Character: ● Self   ● Other: _____
Your Role: ● Participant ● Observer
Colors: ● B&W   ● Vivid   ● Muted   Color/s: _____

Location: _____

What's in the Background? _____

Emotions During the Dream:	Emotions Upon Awakening:
● Fear ● Dread	● Fear ● Dread
● Joy ● Excitement	● Joy ● Excitement
● Other_____	● Other_____

What's the Dream About?

List or Sketch Important Symbols

Pray for the Interpretation

Your Personal Dream Journal

My Reflections

Continued

Notable Events Going on at this Time

Sandie Freed

My Dream

Date: ▓▓▓▓ Time: ▓▓▓▓ Recurring? ▓▓▓▓ When? ▓▓▓▓
Dream Title:
▓▓▓▓▓▓▓▓▓▓▓▓▓▓▓▓▓▓▓▓▓▓▓▓▓▓▓▓▓▓▓▓▓▓

Main Character: ● Self   ● Other: _____
Your Role: ● Participant ● Observer
Colors: ● B&W   ● Vivid   ● Muted   Color/s: _____

Location: _____

What's in the Background? _____

Emotions During the Dream: | Emotions Upon Awakening:
● Fear ● Dread | ● Fear ● Dread
● Joy   ● Excitement | ● Joy   ● Excitement
● Other_____ | ● Other_____

What's the Dream About?

List or Sketch Important Symbols

Pray for the Interpretation

Your Personal Dream Journal

My Reflections

Continued

Notable Events Going on at this Time

Sandie Freed

My Dream

Date: ⬛ Time: ⬛ Recurring? ⬛ When? ⬛
Dream Title:
⬛

Main Character: ● Self ● Other: _____
Your Role: ● Participant ● Observer
Colors: ● B&W ● Vivid ● Muted Color/s: _____

Location: _____

What's in the Background? _____

Emotions During the Dream: | Emotions Upon Awakening:
  ● Fear ● Dread | ● Fear ● Dread
  ● Joy   ● Excitement | ● Joy   ● Excitement
  ● Other_____ | ● Other_____

What's the Dream About?

List or Sketch Important Symbols

Pray for the Interpretation

Your Personal Dream Journal

My Reflections

Continued

Notable Events Going on at this Time

Sandie Freed

My Dream

Date: ▇▇▇▇▇ Time: ▇▇▇▇▇ Recurring? ▇▇▇▇▇ When? ▇▇▇▇▇
Dream Title:
▇▇▇▇▇▇▇▇▇▇▇▇▇▇▇▇▇▇▇▇▇▇▇▇▇▇▇▇▇▇▇▇▇▇▇▇

Main Character: ● Self   ● Other: _____
Your Role: ● Participant ● Observer
Colors: ● B&W   ● Vivid   ● Muted   Color/s: _____

Location: _____

What's in the Background? _____

Emotions During the Dream:	Emotions Upon Awakening:
● Fear ● Dread	● Fear ● Dread
● Joy ● Excitement	● Joy ● Excitement
● Other_____	● Other_____

What's the Dream About?

List or Sketch Important Symbols

Pray for the Interpretation

Your Personal Dream Journal

My Reflections

Continued

Notable Events Going on at this Time

Sandie Freed

My Dream

Date: _____ Time: _____ Recurring? _____ When? _____
Dream Title:
_____

Main Character: ● Self   ● Other: _____
Your Role: ● Participant ● Observer
Colors: ● B&W   ● Vivid   ● Muted   Color/s: _____

Location: _____

What's in the Background? _____

Emotions During the Dream: Emotions Upon Awakening:
  ● Fear   ● Dread   ● Fear   ● Dread
  ● Joy   ● Excitement   ● Joy   ● Excitement
  ● Other_____   ● Other_____

What's the Dream About?

List or Sketch Important Symbols

Pray for the Interpretation

45

Your Personal Dream Journal

My Reflections

Continued

Notable Events Going on at this Time

Sandie Freed

My Dream

Date: _____ Time: _____ Recurring? _____ When? _____
Dream Title:
_____

Main Character: ● Self   ● Other: _____
Your Role: ● Participant ● Observer
Colors: ● B&W   ● Vivid   ● Muted   Color/s: _____

Location: _____

What's in the Background? _____

Emotions During the Dream:	Emotions Upon Awakening:
● Fear ● Dread	● Fear ● Dread
● Joy ● Excitement	● Joy ● Excitement
● Other_____	● Other_____

What's the Dream About?

List or Sketch Important Symbols

Pray for the Interpretation

Your Personal Dream Journal

My Reflections

Continued

Notable Events Going on at this Time

Sandie Freed

My Dream

Date: _____ Time: _____ Recurring? _____ When? _____
Dream Title:
_____

Main Character: ● Self   ● Other: _____
Your Role: ● Participant   ● Observer
Colors: ● B&W   ● Vivid   ● Muted   Color/s: _____

Location: _____

What's in the Background? _____

Emotions During the Dream: Emotions Upon Awakening:
  ● Fear   ● Dread   ● Fear   ● Dread
  ● Joy   ● Excitement   ● Joy   ● Excitement
  ● Other_____   ● Other_____

What's the Dream About?

List or Sketch Important Symbols

Pray for the Interpretation

Your Personal Dream Journal

My Reflections

Continued

Notable Events Going on at this Time

Sandie Freed

My Dream

Date: ▭ Time: ▭ Recurring? ▭ When? ▭
Dream Title:
▭

Main Character: ● Self ● Other: _____
Your Role: ● Participant ● Observer
Colors: ● B&W ● Vivid ● Muted Color/s: _____

Location: _____

What's in the Background? _____

Emotions During the Dream: Emotions Upon Awakening:
  ● Fear   ● Dread   ● Fear   ● Dread
  ● Joy   ● Excitement   ● Joy   ● Excitement
  ● Other_____   ● Other_____

What's the Dream About?

List or Sketch Important Symbols

Pray for the Interpretation

Your Personal Dream Journal

My Reflections

Continued

Notable Events Going on at this Time

Sandie Freed

My Dream

Date: _____ Time: _____ Recurring? _____ When? _____
Dream Title:
_____

Main Character: ● Self   ● Other: _____
Your Role: ● Participant ● Observer
Colors: ● B&W   ● Vivid   ● Muted   Color/s: _____

Location: _____

What's in the Background? _____

Emotions During the Dream: Emotions Upon Awakening:
   ● Fear   ● Dread   ● Fear   ● Dread
   ● Joy   ● Excitement   ● Joy   ● Excitement
   ● Other_____   ● Other_____

What's the Dream About?

List or Sketch Important Symbols

Pray for the Interpretation

Your Personal Dream Journal

My Reflections

Continued

Notable Events Going on at this Time

Sandie Freed

My Dream

Date: _____ Time: _____ Recurring? _____ When? _____
Dream Title: _____
_____

Main Character: ● Self   ● Other: _____
Your Role: ● Participant ● Observer
Colors: ● B&W   ● Vivid   ● Muted   Color/s: _____

Location: _____

What's in the Background? _____

Emotions During the Dream: Emotions Upon Awakening:
  ● Fear   ● Dread   ● Fear   ● Dread
  ● Joy   ● Excitement   ● Joy   ● Excitement
  ● Other_____   ● Other_____

What's the Dream About?

List or Sketch Important Symbols

Pray for the Interpretation

My Reflections

Continued

Notable Events Going on at this Time

Sandie Freed

My Dream

Date: ⬤　　　Time: ⬤　　　Recurring? ⬤　　　When? ⬤
Dream Title:

Main Character: ⬤ Self　　⬤ Other: _____
Your Role:　　　⬤ Participant　⬤ Observer
Colors: ⬤ B&W　⬤ Vivid　　⬤ Muted　Color/s: _____

Location: _____

What's in the Background? _____

Emotions During the Dream:　　　｜　Emotions Upon Awakening:
　⬤ Fear　⬤ Dread　　　　　　｜　　⬤ Fear　⬤ Dread
　⬤ Joy　⬤ Excitement　　　　｜　　⬤ Joy　⬤ Excitement
　⬤ Other_____　　｜　　⬤ Other_____

What's the Dream About?

List or Sketch Important Symbols

Pray for the Interpretation

Your Personal Dream Journal

My Reflections

Continued

Notable Events Going on at this Time

Sandie Freed

My Dream

Date: ⬤　　　Time: ⬤　　　Recurring? ⬤　　　When? ⬤
Dream Title:
　

Main Character:　⬤ Self　　　⬤ Other: _____
Your Role:　　　⬤ Participant　⬤ Observer
Colors:　⬤ B&W　⬤ Vivid　　　⬤ Muted　Color/s: _____

Location: _____

What's in the Background? _____

Emotions During the Dream:　　　　Emotions Upon Awakening:
　⬤ Fear　⬤ Dread　　　　　　　　⬤ Fear　⬤ Dread
　⬤ Joy　⬤ Excitement　　　　　　⬤ Joy　⬤ Excitement
　⬤ Other_____　　　　　⬤ Other_____

What's the Dream About?

List or Sketch Important Symbols

Pray for the Interpretation

My Reflections

Continued

Notable Events Going on at this Time

Sandie Freed

My Dream

Date: _____ Time: _____ Recurring? _____ When? _____
Dream Title:
_____

Main Character: ● Self   ● Other: _____
Your Role: ● Participant ● Observer
Colors: ● B&W   ● Vivid   ● Muted   Color/s: _____

Location: _____

What's in the Background? _____

Emotions During the Dream: | Emotions Upon Awakening:
 ● Fear   ● Dread | ● Fear   ● Dread
 ● Joy   ● Excitement | ● Joy   ● Excitement
 ● Other_____ | ● Other_____

What's the Dream About?

List or Sketch Important Symbols

Pray for the Interpretation

Your Personal Dream Journal

My Reflections

Continued

Notable Events Going on at this Time

Sandie Freed

My Dream

Date: _____ Time: _____ Recurring? _____ When? _____
Dream Title:
_____

Main Character: ● Self   ● Other: _____
Your Role: ● Participant ● Observer
Colors: ● B&W   ● Vivid   ● Muted   Color/s: _____

Location: _____

What's in the Background? _____

Emotions During the Dream:	Emotions Upon Awakening:
● Fear ● Dread	● Fear ● Dread
● Joy ● Excitement	● Joy ● Excitement
● Other_____	● Other_____

What's the Dream About?

List or Sketch Important Symbols

Pray for the Interpretation

Your Personal Dream Journal

My Reflections

Continued

Notable Events Going on at this Time

Sandie Freed

My Dream

Date: _____ Time: _____ Recurring? _____ When? _____
Dream Title: _____

Main Character: ● Self   ● Other: _____
Your Role: ● Participant ● Observer
Colors: ● B&W   ● Vivid   ● Muted   Color/s: _____

Location: _____

What's in the Background? _____

Emotions During the Dream:	Emotions Upon Awakening:
● Fear ● Dread	● Fear ● Dread
● Joy ● Excitement	● Joy ● Excitement
● Other_____	● Other_____

What's the Dream About?

List or Sketch Important Symbols

Pray for the Interpretation

Your Personal Dream Journal

My Reflections

Continued

Notable Events Going on at this Time

Sandie Freed

My Dream

Date: _____ Time: _____ Recurring? _____ When? _____
Dream Title:
_____

Main Character: ● Self   ● Other: _____
Your Role: ● Participant ● Observer
Colors: ● B&W   ● Vivid   ● Muted   Color/s: _____

Location: _____

What's in the Background? _____

Emotions During the Dream: Emotions Upon Awakening:
  ● Fear   ● Dread   ● Fear   ● Dread
  ● Joy   ● Excitement   ● Joy   ● Excitement
  ● Other_____   ● Other_____

What's the Dream About?

List or Sketch Important Symbols

Pray for the Interpretation

Your Personal Dream Journal

My Reflections

Continued

Notable Events Going on at this Time

Sandie Freed

My Dream

Date: _____ Time: _____ Recurring? _____ When? _____
Dream Title:
_____

Main Character: ● Self   ● Other: _____
Your Role: ● Participant ● Observer
Colors: ● B&W ● Vivid   ● Muted   Color/s: _____

Location: _____

What's in the Background? _____

Emotions During the Dream: Emotions Upon Awakening:
  ● Fear   ● Dread   ● Fear   ● Dread
  ● Joy   ● Excitement   ● Joy   ● Excitement
  ● Other_____   ● Other_____

What's the Dream About?

List or Sketch Important Symbols

Pray for the Interpretation

Your Personal Dream Journal

My Reflections

Continued

Notable Events Going on at this Time

Sandie Freed

My Dream

Date: _____ Time: _____ Recurring? _____ When? _____
Dream Title:
_____

Main Character: ● Self   ● Other: _____
Your Role: ● Participant ● Observer
Colors: ● B&W   ● Vivid   ● Muted   Color/s: _____

Location: _____

What's in the Background? _____

Emotions During the Dream: Emotions Upon Awakening:
  ● Fear   ● Dread   ● Fear   ● Dread
  ● Joy   ● Excitement   ● Joy   ● Excitement
  ● Other_____   ● Other_____

What's the Dream About?

List or Sketch Important Symbols

Pray for the Interpretation

Your Personal Dream Journal

My Reflections

Continued

Notable Events Going on at this Time

Sandie Freed

My Dream

Date: ▨▨▨▨▨   Time: ▨▨▨▨▨   Recurring? ▨▨▨▨   When? ▨▨▨▨
Dream Title:
▨▨▨▨▨▨▨▨▨▨▨▨▨▨▨▨▨▨▨▨▨▨▨▨▨▨▨▨▨▨▨

Main Character: ● Self   ● Other: _____
Your Role: ● Participant   ● Observer
Colors: ● B&W   ● Vivid   ● Muted   Color/s: _____

Location: _____

What's in the Background? _____

Emotions During the Dream:	Emotions Upon Awakening:
● Fear ● Dread	● Fear ● Dread
● Joy ● Excitement	● Joy ● Excitement
● Other_____	● Other_____

What's the Dream About?

List or Sketch Important Symbols

Pray for the Interpretation

Your Personal Dream Journal

My Reflections

Continued

Notable Events Going on at this Time

Sandie Freed

My Dream

Date: _____ Time: _____ Recurring? _____ When? _____
Dream Title:
_____

Main Character: ● Self   ● Other: _____
Your Role: ● Participant ● Observer
Colors: ● B&W   ● Vivid   ● Muted   Color/s: _____

Location: _____

What's in the Background? _____

Emotions During the Dream:	Emotions Upon Awakening:
● Fear ● Dread	● Fear ● Dread
● Joy ● Excitement	● Joy ● Excitement
● Other_____	● Other_____

What's the Dream About?

List or Sketch Important Symbols

Pray for the Interpretation

Your Personal Dream Journal

My Reflections

Continued

Notable Events Going on at this Time

Sandie Freed

My Dream

Date: _____ Time: _____ Recurring? _____ When? _____

Dream Title:
_____

Main Character: ● Self   ● Other: _____
Your Role: ● Participant ● Observer
Colors: ● B&W   ● Vivid   ● Muted   Color/s: _____

Location: _____

What's in the Background? _____

Emotions During the Dream:	Emotions Upon Awakening:
● Fear ● Dread	● Fear ● Dread
● Joy ● Excitement	● Joy ● Excitement
● Other_____	● Other_____

What's the Dream About?

List or Sketch Important Symbols

Pray for the Interpretation

Your Personal Dream Journal

My Reflections

Continued

Notable Events Going on at this Time

Sandie Freed

My Dream

Date: ▇▇▇▇ Time: ▇▇▇ Recurring? ▇▇▇ When? ▇▇▇
Dream Title:
▇▇▇▇▇▇▇▇▇▇▇▇▇▇▇▇▇▇▇▇▇▇▇▇▇▇

Main Character: ● Self   ● Other: _____
Your Role: ● Participant ● Observer
Colors: ● B&W   ● Vivid   ● Muted   Color/s: _____

Location: _____

What's in the Background? _____

Emotions During the Dream:	Emotions Upon Awakening:
● Fear ● Dread	● Fear ● Dread
● Joy ● Excitement	● Joy ● Excitement
● Other_____	● Other_____

What's the Dream About?

List or Sketch Important Symbols

Pray for the Interpretation

Your Personal Dream Journal

My Reflections

Continued

Notable Events Going on at this Time

Sandie Freed

My Dream

Date: ▬▬▬ Time: ▬▬▬ Recurring? ▬▬▬ When? ▬▬▬
Dream Title:
▬▬▬▬▬▬▬▬▬▬▬▬▬▬▬▬▬▬▬▬

Main Character: ● Self   ● Other: _____
Your Role: ● Participant ● Observer
Colors: ● B&W ● Vivid   ● Muted   Color/s: _____

Location: _____

What's in the Background? _____

Emotions During the Dream:	Emotions Upon Awakening:
● Fear ● Dread	● Fear ● Dread
● Joy ● Excitement	● Joy ● Excitement
● Other_____	● Other_____

What's the Dream About?

List or Sketch Important Symbols

Pray for the Interpretation

Your Personal Dream Journal

My Reflections

Continued

Notable Events Going on at this Time

Sandie Freed

My Dream

Date: _____ Time: _____ Recurring? _____ When? _____
Dream Title:
_____

Main Character: ● Self   ● Other: _____
Your Role: ● Participant ● Observer
Colors: ● B&W   ● Vivid   ● Muted   Color/s: _____

Location: _____

What's in the Background? _____

Emotions During the Dream: Emotions Upon Awakening:
  ● Fear   ● Dread   ● Fear   ● Dread
  ● Joy   ● Excitement   ● Joy   ● Excitement
  ● Other_____   ● Other_____

What's the Dream About?

List or Sketch Important Symbols

Pray for the Interpretation

Your Personal Dream Journal

My Reflections

Continued

Notable Events Going on at this Time

Sandie Freed

My Dream

Date: ⬤   Time: ⬤   Recurring? ⬤   When? ⬤
Dream Title:
⬤

Main Character: ⬤ Self   ⬤ Other: _____
Your Role: ⬤ Participant   ⬤ Observer
Colors: ⬤ B&W   ⬤ Vivid   ⬤ Muted   Color/s: _____

Location: _____

What's in the Background? _____

Emotions During the Dream: Emotions Upon Awakening:
  ⬤ Fear   ⬤ Dread   ⬤ Fear   ⬤ Dread
  ⬤ Joy   ⬤ Excitement   ⬤ Joy   ⬤ Excitement
  ⬤ Other_____   ⬤ Other_____

What's the Dream About?

List or Sketch Important Symbols

Pray for the Interpretation

Your Personal Dream Journal

My Reflections

Continued

Notable Events Going on at this Time

Sandie Freed

My Dream

Date: ▭ Time: ▭ Recurring? ▭ When? ▭
Dream Title:
▬▬▬▬▬▬▬▬▬▬▬▬▬▬▬▬▬▬

Main Character: ● Self   ● Other: _____
Your Role: ● Participant ● Observer
Colors: ● B&W   ● Vivid   ● Muted   Color/s: _____

Location: _____

What's in the Background? _____

Emotions During the Dream:	Emotions Upon Awakening:
● Fear ● Dread	● Fear ● Dread
● Joy ● Excitement	● Joy ● Excitement
● Other_____	● Other_____

What's the Dream About?

List or Sketch Important Symbols

Pray for the Interpretation

Your Personal Dream Journal

My Reflections

Continued

Notable Events Going on at this Time

Sandie Freed

My Dream

Date: _____ Time: _____ Recurring? _____ When? _____
Dream Title:
_____

Main Character: ● Self   ● Other: _____
Your Role: ● Participant ● Observer
Colors: ● B&W   ● Vivid   ● Muted   Color/s: _____

Location: _____

What's in the Background? _____

Emotions During the Dream: Emotions Upon Awakening:
   ● Fear   ● Dread   ● Fear   ● Dread
   ● Joy   ● Excitement   ● Joy   ● Excitement
   ● Other_____   ● Other_____

What's the Dream About?

List or Sketch Important Symbols

Pray for the Interpretation

Your Personal Dream Journal

My Reflections

Continued

Notable Events Going on at this Time

Sandie Freed

My Dream

Date: ▬▬▬▬ Time: ▬▬▬ Recurring? ▬▬▬ When? ▬▬▬
Dream Title:
▬▬▬▬▬▬▬▬▬▬▬▬▬▬▬▬▬▬▬▬▬▬▬▬▬▬

Main Character: ● Self   ● Other: _____
Your Role: ● Participant ● Observer
Colors: ● B&W   ● Vivid   ● Muted   Color/s: _____

Location: _____

What's in the Background? _____

Emotions During the Dream: | Emotions Upon Awakening:
● Fear ● Dread | ● Fear ● Dread
● Joy   ● Excitement | ● Joy   ● Excitement
● Other_____ | ● Other_____

What's the Dream About?

List or Sketch Important Symbols

Pray for the Interpretation

Your Personal Dream Journal

My Reflections

Continued

Notable Events Going on at this Time

Sandie Freed

My Dream

Date: _____ Time: _____ Recurring? _____ When? _____
Dream Title:
_____

Main Character: ● Self   ● Other: _____
Your Role: ● Participant ● Observer
Colors: ● B&W   ● Vivid   ● Muted   Color/s: _____

Location: _____

What's in the Background? _____

Emotions During the Dream: | Emotions Upon Awakening:
● Fear   ● Dread | ● Fear   ● Dread
● Joy   ● Excitement | ● Joy   ● Excitement
● Other_____ | ● Other_____

What's the Dream About?

List or Sketch Important Symbols

Pray for the Interpretation

Your Personal Dream Journal

My Reflections

Continued

Notable Events Going on at this Time

Sandie Freed

My Dream

Date: _____ Time: _____ Recurring? _____ When? _____
Dream Title:
_____

Main Character: ● Self   ● Other: _____
Your Role: ● Participant ● Observer
Colors: ● B&W   ● Vivid   ● Muted   Color/s: _____

Location: _____

What's in the Background? _____

Emotions During the Dream:	Emotions Upon Awakening:
● Fear ● Dread	● Fear ● Dread
● Joy ● Excitement	● Joy ● Excitement
● Other_____	● Other_____

What's the Dream About?

List or Sketch Important Symbols

Pray for the Interpretation

Your Personal Dream Journal

My Reflections

Continued

Notable Events Going on at this Time

Sandie Freed

My Dream

Date: _____ Time: _____ Recurring? _____ When? _____
Dream Title:
_____

Main Character: ● Self   ● Other: _____
Your Role: ● Participant ● Observer
Colors: ● B&W ● Vivid   ● Muted   Color/s: _____

Location: _____

What's in the Background? _____

Emotions During the Dream:	Emotions Upon Awakening:
● Fear ● Dread	● Fear ● Dread
● Joy ● Excitement	● Joy ● Excitement
● Other_____	● Other_____

What's the Dream About?

List or Sketch Important Symbols

Pray for the Interpretation

Your Personal Dream Journal

My Reflections

Continued

Notable Events Going on at this Time

Sandie Freed

My Dream

Date: ▓▓▓▓   Time: ▓▓▓▓   Recurring? ▓▓▓▓   When? ▓▓▓▓
Dream Title:
▓▓▓▓▓▓▓▓▓▓▓▓▓▓▓▓▓▓▓▓▓▓▓▓▓▓▓▓▓▓▓▓▓▓▓▓

Main Character: ● Self   ● Other: _____
Your Role: ● Participant   ● Observer
Colors: ● B&W   ● Vivid   ● Muted   Color/s: _____

Location: _____

What's in the Background? _____

Emotions During the Dream: | Emotions Upon Awakening:
● Fear ● Dread | ● Fear ● Dread
● Joy   ● Excitement | ● Joy   ● Excitement
● Other_____ | ● Other_____

What's the Dream About?

List or Sketch Important Symbols

Pray for the Interpretation

Your Personal Dream Journal

My Reflections

Continued

Notable Events Going on at this Time

Sandie Freed

My Dream

Date: ▇▇▇ Time: ▇▇▇ Recurring? ▇▇▇ When? ▇▇▇
Dream Title:
▇▇▇▇▇▇▇▇▇▇▇▇▇▇▇▇▇▇▇▇▇▇▇▇▇▇▇▇▇▇▇▇

Main Character: ● Self   ● Other: _____
Your Role: ● Participant ● Observer
Colors: ● B&W   ● Vivid   ● Muted   Color/s: _____

Location: _____

What's in the Background? _____

Emotions During the Dream: Emotions Upon Awakening:
  ● Fear   ● Dread   ● Fear   ● Dread
  ● Joy   ● Excitement   ● Joy   ● Excitement
  ● Other_____   ● Other_____

What's the Dream About?

List or Sketch Important Symbols

Pray for the Interpretation

Your Personal Dream Journal

My Reflections

Continued

Notable Events Going on at this Time

Sandie Freed

My Dream

Date: _____ Time: _____ Recurring? _____ When? _____
Dream Title:
_____

Main Character: ● Self   ● Other: _____
Your Role: ● Participant ● Observer
Colors: ● B&W   ● Vivid   ● Muted   Color/s: _____

Location: _____

What's in the Background? _____

Emotions During the Dream: Emotions Upon Awakening:
　● Fear   ● Dread   　● Fear   ● Dread
　● Joy   ● Excitement   　● Joy   ● Excitement
　● Other_____   　● Other_____

What's the Dream About?

List or Sketch Important Symbols

Pray for the Interpretation

Your Personal Dream Journal

My Reflections

Continued

Notable Events Going on at this Time

Sandie Freed

My Dream

Date: _____ Time: _____ Recurring? _____ When? _____
Dream Title:
_____

Main Character: ● Self   ● Other: _____
Your Role: ● Participant ● Observer
Colors: ● B&W   ● Vivid   ● Muted   Color/s: _____

Location: _____

What's in the Background? _____

Emotions During the Dream: | Emotions Upon Awakening:
● Fear   ● Dread | ● Fear   ● Dread
● Joy   ● Excitement | ● Joy   ● Excitement
● Other_____ | ● Other_____

What's the Dream About?

List or Sketch Important Symbols

Pray for the Interpretation

Your Personal Dream Journal

My Reflections

Continued

Notable Events Going on at this Time

Sandie Freed

My Dream

Date: _____ Time: _____ Recurring? _____ When? _____
Dream Title:
_____

Main Character: ● Self   ● Other: _____
Your Role: ● Participant ● Observer
Colors: ● B&W   ● Vivid   ● Muted   Color/s: _____

Location: _____

What's in the Background? _____

Emotions During the Dream: Emotions Upon Awakening:
  ● Fear   ● Dread   ● Fear   ● Dread
  ● Joy   ● Excitement   ● Joy   ● Excitement
  ● Other_____   ● Other_____

What's the Dream About?

List or Sketch Important Symbols

Pray for the Interpretation

Your Personal Dream Journal

My Reflections

Continued

Notable Events Going on at this Time

Sandie Freed

My Dream

Date: ▬▬▬▬ Time: ▬▬▬▬ Recurring? ▬▬▬▬ When? ▬▬▬▬
Dream Title:
▬▬▬▬▬▬▬▬▬▬▬▬▬▬▬▬▬▬▬▬▬▬▬▬▬▬▬▬▬▬▬▬▬▬

Main Character: ● Self   ● Other: _____
Your Role: ● Participant ● Observer
Colors: ● B&W   ● Vivid   ● Muted   Color/s: _____

Location: _____

What's in the Background? _____

Emotions During the Dream: Emotions Upon Awakening:
　● Fear   ● Dread   　● Fear   ● Dread
　● Joy   ● Excitement   　● Joy   ● Excitement
　● Other_____   　● Other_____

What's the Dream About?

List or Sketch Important Symbols

Pray for the Interpretation

Your Personal Dream Journal

My Reflections

Continued

Notable Events Going on at this Time

Sandie Freed

My Dream

Date: _____ Time: _____ Recurring? _____ When? _____
Dream Title:
_____

Main Character: ● Self   ● Other: _____
Your Role: ● Participant ● Observer
Colors: ● B&W   ● Vivid   ● Muted   Color/s: _____

Location: _____

What's in the Background? _____

Emotions During the Dream:	Emotions Upon Awakening:
● Fear ● Dread	● Fear ● Dread
● Joy ● Excitement	● Joy ● Excitement
● Other_____	● Other_____

What's the Dream About?

List or Sketch Important Symbols

Pray for the Interpretation

Your Personal Dream Journal

My Reflections

Continued

Notable Events Going on at this Time

Sandie Freed

My Dream

Date: _____ Time: _____ Recurring? _____ When? _____
Dream Title: _____

Main Character: ● Self   ● Other: _____
Your Role: ● Participant ● Observer
Colors: ● B&W   ● Vivid   ● Muted   Color/s: _____

Location: _____

What's in the Background? _____

Emotions During the Dream: Emotions Upon Awakening:
   ● Fear   ● Dread   ● Fear   ● Dread
   ● Joy   ● Excitement   ● Joy   ● Excitement
   ● Other_____   ● Other_____

What's the Dream About?

List or Sketch Important Symbols

Pray for the Interpretation

Your Personal Dream Journal

My Reflections

Continued

Notable Events Going on at this Time

Sandie Freed

My Dream

Date: _____ Time: _____ Recurring? _____ When? _____
Dream Title:
_____

Main Character: ● Self   ● Other: _____
Your Role: ● Participant ● Observer
Colors: ● B&W   ● Vivid   ● Muted   Color/s: _____

Location: _____

What's in the Background? _____

Emotions During the Dream:	Emotions Upon Awakening:
● Fear ● Dread	● Fear ● Dread
● Joy ● Excitement	● Joy ● Excitement
● Other_____	● Other_____

What's the Dream About?

List or Sketch Important Symbols

Pray for the Interpretation

Your Personal Dream Journal

My Reflections

Continued

Notable Events Going on at this Time

Sandie Freed

My Dream

Date: _____ Time: _____ Recurring? _____ When? _____
Dream Title: _____

Main Character: ● Self   ● Other: _____
Your Role: ● Participant   ● Observer
Colors: ● B&W   ● Vivid   ● Muted   Color/s: _____

Location: _____

What's in the Background? _____

Emotions During the Dream: Emotions Upon Awakening:
  ● Fear   ● Dread   ● Fear   ● Dread
  ● Joy   ● Excitement   ● Joy   ● Excitement
  ● Other_____   ● Other_____

What's the Dream About?

List or Sketch Important Symbols

Pray for the Interpretation

Your Personal Dream Journal

My Reflections

Continued

Notable Events Going on at this Time

Sandie Freed

My Dream

Date: _____ Time: _____ Recurring? _____ When? _____
Dream Title:
_____

Main Character: ● Self   ● Other: _____
Your Role: ● Participant   ● Observer
Colors: ● B&W   ● Vivid   ● Muted   Color/s: _____

Location: _____

What's in the Background? _____

Emotions During the Dream: | Emotions Upon Awakening:
  ● Fear   ● Dread | ● Fear   ● Dread
  ● Joy   ● Excitement | ● Joy   ● Excitement
  ● Other_____ | ● Other_____

What's the Dream About?

List or Sketch Important Symbols

Pray for the Interpretation

Your Personal Dream Journal

My Reflections

Continued

Notable Events Going on at this Time

Sandie Freed

My Dream

Date: ▇▇▇▇ Time: ▇▇▇▇ Recurring? ▇▇▇▇ When? ▇▇▇▇
Dream Title:
▇▇▇▇▇▇▇▇▇▇▇▇▇▇▇▇▇▇▇▇▇▇▇▇▇▇▇▇▇▇▇▇▇▇

Main Character: ● Self   ● Other: _____
Your Role: ● Participant ● Observer
Colors: ● B&W   ● Vivid   ● Muted   Color/s: _____

Location: _____

What's in the Background? _____

Emotions During the Dream: | Emotions Upon Awakening:
  ● Fear   ● Dread | ● Fear   ● Dread
  ● Joy   ● Excitement | ● Joy   ● Excitement
  ● Other_____ | ● Other_____

What's the Dream About?

List or Sketch Important Symbols

Pray for the Interpretation

Your Personal Dream Journal

My Reflections

Continued

Notable Events Going on at this Time

Sandie Freed

My Dream

Date: _____ Time: _____ Recurring? _____ When? _____
Dream Title: _____
_____

Main Character: ● Self   ● Other: _____
Your Role: ● Participant ● Observer
Colors: ● B&W   ● Vivid   ● Muted   Color/s: _____

Location: _____

What's in the Background? _____

Emotions During the Dream:	Emotions Upon Awakening:
● Fear ● Dread	● Fear ● Dread
● Joy ● Excitement	● Joy ● Excitement
● Other_____	● Other_____

What's the Dream About?

List or Sketch Important Symbols

Pray for the Interpretation

123

Your Personal Dream Journal

My Reflections

Continued

Notable Events Going on at this Time

Sandie Freed

My Dream

Date: _____ Time: _____ Recurring? _____ When? _____
Dream Title:
_____

Main Character: ● Self   ● Other: _____
Your Role: ● Participant ● Observer
Colors: ● B&W ● Vivid   ● Muted   Color/s: _____

Location: _____

What's in the Background? _____

Emotions During the Dream: | Emotions Upon Awakening:
● Fear   ● Dread | ● Fear   ● Dread
● Joy   ● Excitement | ● Joy   ● Excitement
● Other_____ | ● Other_____

What's the Dream About?

List or Sketch Important Symbols

Pray for the Interpretation

Your Personal Dream Journal

My Reflections

Continued

Notable Events Going on at this Time

Sandie Freed Books

Understanding Your Dreams—How to Unlock the Meaning of God's Messages

Spoken in the language of heaven—the language of our spirits—dreams and visions can be revelations from God that connect straight to your heart. He can use them to reveal your future, heal your soul, draw you closer to Him, impart direction and guidance, expose and defeat strongholds, and empower you to step into your true purpose and destiny.

Laying out a biblical framework for interpreting these nighttime messages, pastor and author Sandie Freed helps you translate this beautiful language and discover how to: prepare to hear from God, discern the source of your dreams, protect, battle and bless your dreams, apply God's messages to your life, empower your children to understand their dreams, and more!
ISBN: 978-0800794200   Chosen Books

Dreams Companion Study Guide

In this companion study guide to *Understanding Your Dreams*, you will find thirteen lessons for *individual or group study*. You will be asked to journal your dreams, use colors to express your emotions, study the Bible verses, answer the questions, fill in the blanks, share your study points with others, and meditate on the message. Through this exhaustive study, Dr. Freed invites you to enter into this mysterious world to find a place where God wishes to speak to you. Size: 8.5x11, perfect bound.
ISBN: 978-1602730618   Parsons Publishing House

Your Personal Dream Journal

ISBN: 978-1602731035   Perfect Bound   Parsons Publishing House
ISBN: 978-1602731042   Coil Bound   Parsons Publishing House